Jumping Doubt

Finding Hope in a World of Faults

Jumping Doubt

Finding Hope in a World of Faults

Marc C. Ness

An Equine Press Book

ISBN: 0692829415
ISBN 13: 978-0692829417

To Graziella and Luna, your willingness to face doubt at the base of a standard gave me a new meaning of hope. This book is for you.

Contents

Introduction

The quest for joy.

The poems in this book speak in various ways about jumping horses. They draw from the essence of training lessons, competitive events, and stories I have had the privilege to be a part of in the presence of jumpers. They are formed around a single idea, that every jumper faces doubt. It is not my intention to cause the reader to focus on uncertainty, but rather to expose it, bring it out of its darkened cage, connect it to other ideas, and transform it into hope.

Hope is a higher state of being that transcends all suffering; it is an outcome based on certainty. It is the inti-thesis of doubt. Jumpers live on hope; they plant seeds of certainty as they turn up the arena, jumping over doubt, rising above personal limits, expecting to feel the exaltation of joy.

The life of a jumper is the quest for joy, the union of friendship between a horse and human. Jumpers form bonds inside the arena at the base of a standard, where horse and human make the vital decision to sacrifice their doubt, rise above the rails, and radiate the sun of their friendship. It is the transcendent act of sacrifice, even above the worldly gifts of winning, that jumpers seek.

But relationships are not formed easily, in particular between horse and rider. To know the intention of another, particularly when you speak a different language is frustrating at best. To trust another with your heart, let alone your life is a circumstance not to be taken lightly.

Hope and doubt, like horse and rider, are lovers. They have quarrels, each attempting to maintain the throne of supremacy by forcing their will upon the other. They walk the same ground and share experiences while pleading with the other to abandon their position and trust. But remember, no lover ever found trust in another's smile, harsh words, and broken promises form the basis for growth. Trust in another is built on quarrels and resolution, not from the mere wish of a lover's kiss.

Poetic analogies, however, are not enough to raise one's knowledge to the heights of wisdom. Real gains in life are found at our feet, on the ground of experience, by facing head on the harsh realities of life. And so, it is with jumpers, as they continue their search for the essence of that glorious, terrifying moment when horse and rider abandon doubt, reach for hope, and trust each other so completely they find union in the sky.

It is my hope this book aids in that discovery.

Marc C. Ness

Acknowledgement

As I was writing this book, I often thought of the endless conversations that took place over the last several years with all my equestrian friends. The experiences we shared have made an indelible mark on my mind. Your courage and compassion in the jumping arena gave me the inspiration for this book.

Although you are too numerous to mention, rest assured, every one of you influenced my ideas. Without you and your horses, I could not have written these poems. Thank you for sharing your equestrian heart.

"Doubt surrounds the human condition,

it teases hope to set our minds free."

A Full Barn

Jumping horses is a full barn,
every stall a new being.

A saint, a warrior, a lover,
all wanting to take the lead.

The edge of hope at the base
of a standard. It's too late to wish
for the warrior, the lovers' here now.

Soft kisses are not what I need,
in too deep for a heart to heart.

Shout a prayer for the saint to assist,
grateful again for a full barn.

Above the Rails

We are here above the rails

contained inside of time,

where love is.

Up here in this sky freedom,

there is no cost to live. There is

only You and I.

This perfect equine union.

You and I.

Equine Constellations

There is no you and I; there is only breathing

inside this equine universe.

You create constellations that light

an arc over shadowed rails.

There is no distance between the efforts,

light years come to the here and now.

Jealousy fills the Milky Way

when hooves leave the ground.

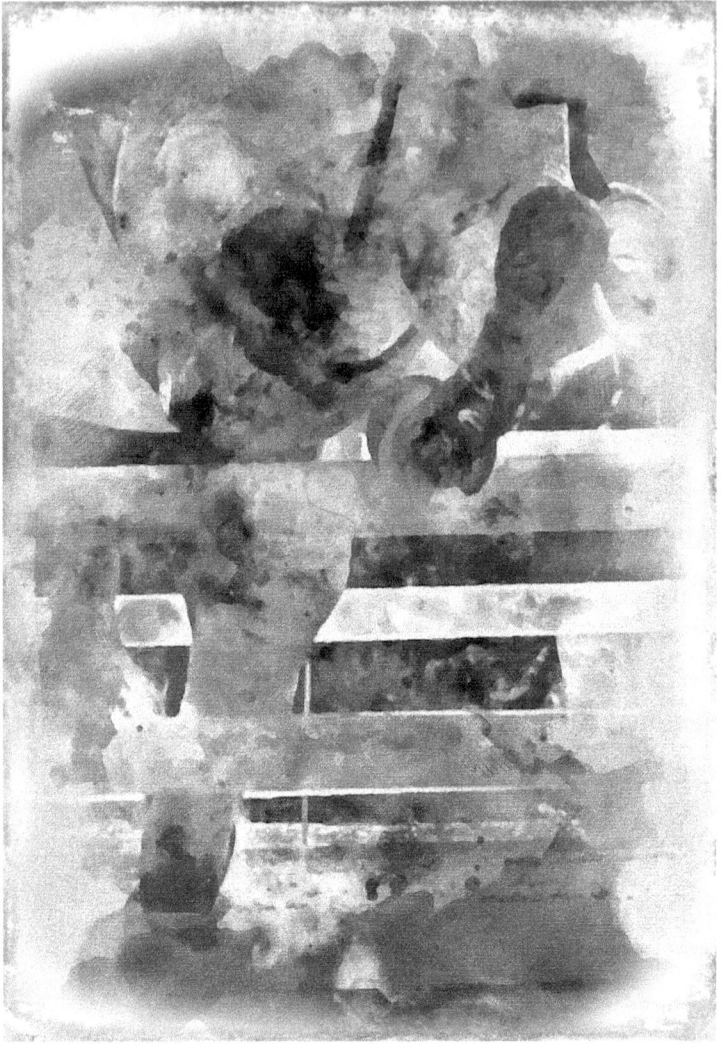

Be a Lighter Load

Let's be real; even friends let each other down.

But there is always forgiveness, the salve

that heals a blistered hoof.

Rely on your friendship but tie your horse.

Wish for the best but drop your fantasy.

There is more to weight than skin and bone;

a broken promise is a heavy burden.

A heavy spirit keeps the body down;

a lighter saddle gives way to flight.

Be a lighter load, a compassionate

spirit weighs less in the saddle.

Find Your Way

As the last rail falls, I cross the finish line,
blaming energy falls over the arena.

This story has been told before,
first, middle, last rail down.

Others come to me for advice, but I
cannot speak for them now.

They must find their own way over doubt.
All I can do is ride my friend to the center
of the storm,

and hope for equine grace.

Half-heartedness

Watch your attitude on the approach,

timid thoughts keep your lover a stride away.

Relying on luck is no way to win a prize,

disappointment lingers on the wrong side of hope.

Bitter hay is less appealing than sweet alfalfa,

the taste of experience confirms the truth.

The champion's life can never rest on half-
heartedness. Hesitation will keep you from

the pure majesty of higher rails.

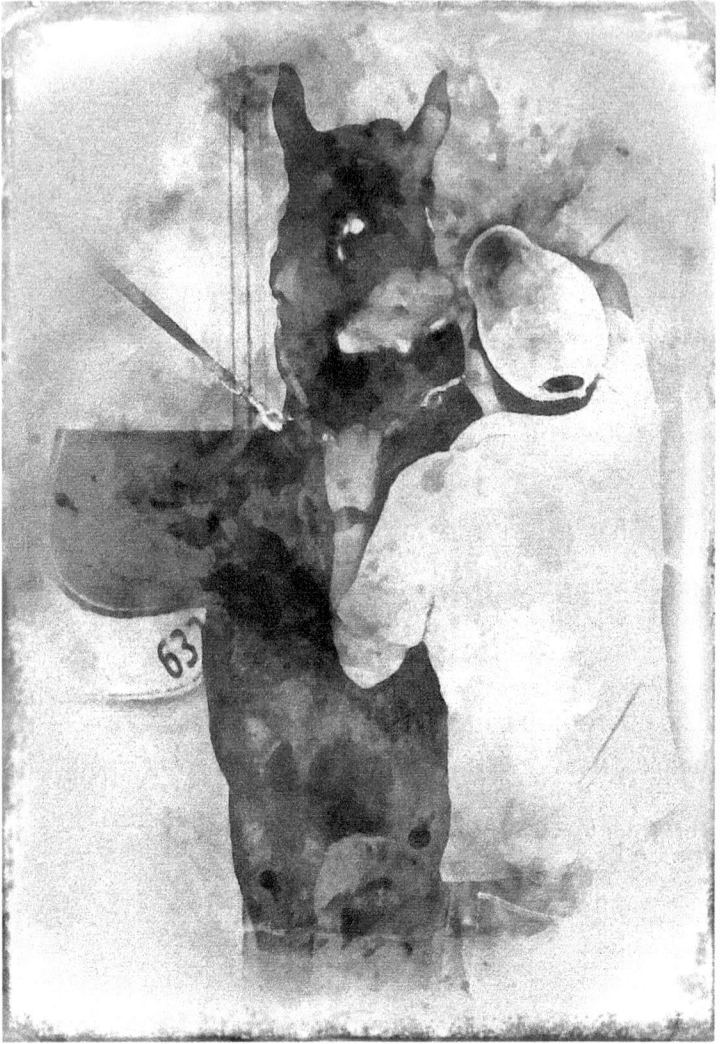

Use the Right Thought

Groom your soul's courage, brush your history clean.

A single grain of sand will make the saddle itch.

Use the right brush, a grander presence appears.

Stroke the wrong direction, a longer time to clean.

The sudden stop leaves a bitter taste.

Another clean round, the sweet taste of victory.

A single doubtful thought and rails begin to fall,

the single clear intention makes smiles at the barn.

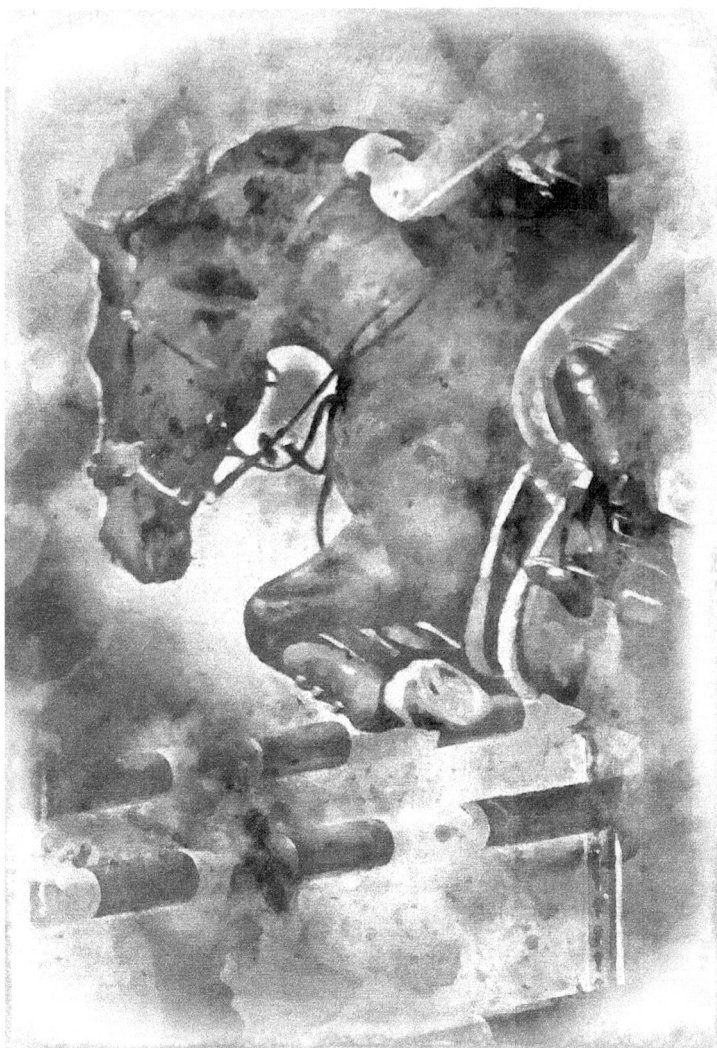

Admire Doubt

The last show I admired hope,

now I canter between the courage.

The last round rails were set on fire,

now the oxer becomes the flame.

My heart is filled with doubt,

smoldering embers in the Liverpool below.

Break the Rules

The old rules govern what we see,
the mare leads, the stallion follows.

The rules inside my head all follow that.
The stern thought chases the kind,
looking for some reward.

This jumping game is all the same.
We leap toward the sky chasing
thoughts of grandeur.

Break the sky bowl and let the grandeur
fall into grandeur. Break all the rules,
leave reward behind.

Without You Here

Without you here soothing my wounds,
I cannot reach the heights of expectation.

All that happens around me falls,
and I become exposed to my own darkness.

Without you here lifting me up,
gravity pulls my thoughts lower.

Without you here rails fall,
as hope defends against hurt
the absence of you.

Without you here.

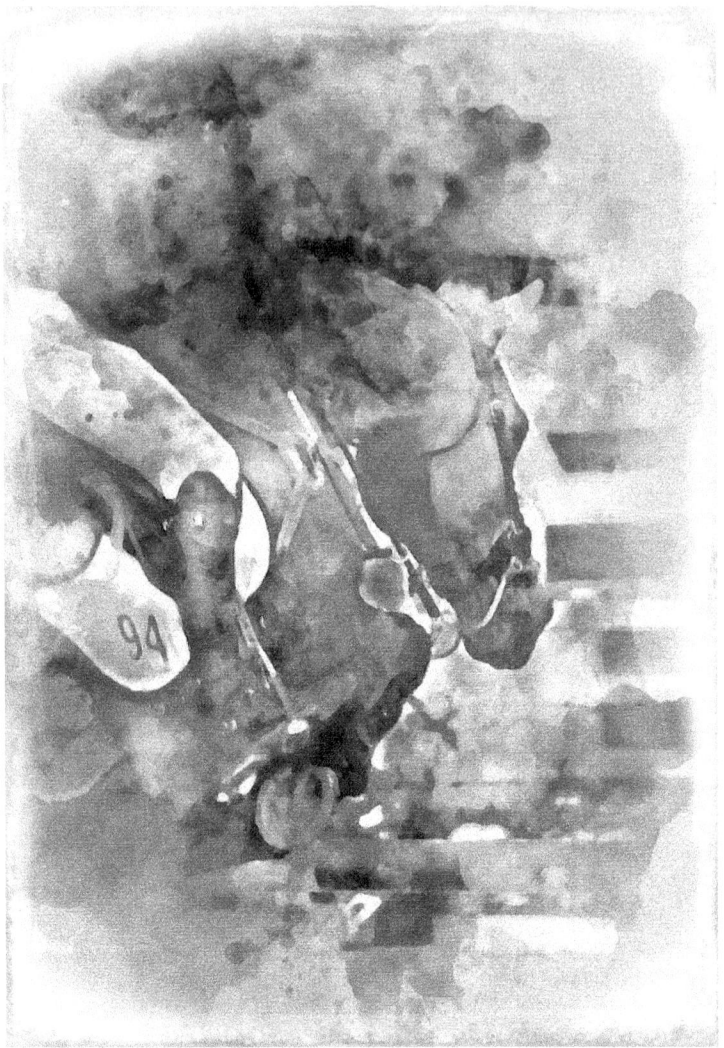

Nothing Left to Lose

Every falling rail becomes a new joy,
the fallen seed breaks free into color.

The barn worm weaves a silk coffin,
stretched wings begin to open
as transformation learns to fly.

A missed distance yields to first place,
yet distance makes the heart grow fonder.

Lost the round and lost my money,
no worries here with nothing left to lose.

Looking Down

Never fight gravity, rails will always fall.

Turn gravity over, leave this world behind.

Jump into the sky-cup, riding on the rim.

Let your doubt spill out, gravity taking over.

Looking down, I feel freedom watching shadows

sliding over rails asking for forgiveness.

Honesty

My whole life spent in lies,

blaming you for second place.

Now is the time for forgiveness,

the rider's way to the jump off.

All you show me is honesty,

the save at the bottom of a hole.

Maybe I'm the one who needs the truth,

not the other way around.

Lies fall like rails as the truth

reveals the honesty beneath.

Saved again by you!

Freedom Across an Oxer

Today I don't care about distance or height,
the time on the clock or my technique.

Today I am the equine soul, the heart
of all horses. I am a traveler of spirit,
where freedom finds its wings across
an oxer.

I'm on my way from the noise of the crowd,
to the silent place where I have
left behind my worries.

Flying high with you inside this
secret equine joy.

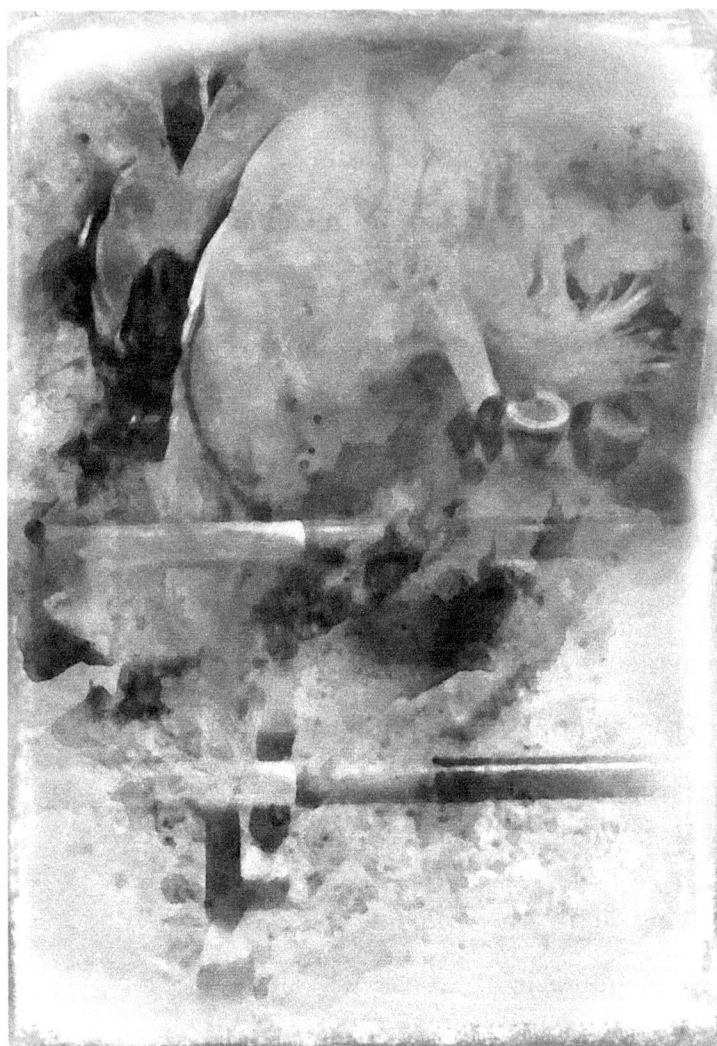

The First Try

What foal ever rose to its feet on the first try?
Its efforts aren't measured that way.

Innocence never springs from definitions,
it follows the joy of freedom.

Leave yesterday's losses behind,
jump the limits of fear like
the foals first try.

Too Many Questions

Real faith comes from madness,

the whirlwind of a fallen rail.

In that moment doubt,

the sound of a heart in question.

Too many questions will set

the heart ablaze.

Whoever finds faith inside the

burning embers, will jump above the flames.

Dragging Doubt

Time to drag the arena,

clear the shadows from your mind.

What do you want?

Falling rails or higher freedom?

Ride the freshly tilled footing

at the start of every gate,

not the heavy heart of shadows past.

No Such Thing as Perfect

There's no such thing as the perfect horse,
you're not perfect either.

This is a game of close enough.

How far over the rails?
Only inches, close enough.

No time faults here.
One second to spare, close enough.

Left your tape measure in the trunk,
missed the distance by half a stride.

Victory comes anyway, close enough!

Your Kingdom

This is your kingdom,

it's the place where you shine.

This is your light,

the ascension toward the clouds.

I try to reach the heights where you reside,

where you jump between the faults.

The best I can offer you,

is to ride with you forever.

Thank you for the ride,

the red carpet whispers through time.

Falling to Glory

This jumping is a calling,
the sound of hooves in my heart.

But this yearning is different,
it's a diamond deep inside the earth,
waiting to burst into color.

False pity has no place in the arena,
that charity gives no advantage.

Human feet walk the earth,
but horse's hooves can fly.

Hidden inside this public arena,
falling rails lead us to glory.

No Turning Back

Will you be with me? At decision time?
When hooves plant firmly?

You know the moment, just the same as I.
There is no turning back the judge's clock,
that plan is passed.

Time is different here, on the edge of
a jumper's life. It's measured by will,
the level of commitment.

The rose opens when the light-hope tells it to,
filling a void with beauty.

This decision is like that. An opening to faith,
where fragrance lets fly, and doubt is left behind.

The Two-Sided Course

Every course has two sides:

One side confidence, the other side doubt.

Not sure what the distance is,

my horse found the stride.

Too quick to ride the downhill seven,

reining in confidence on the two-sided course.

My Heart's Voice

There is a voice that calls from the other side of a
rail, just as grain in a bucket calls the stubborn mare.

Water calls to the journey's thirst,

come back and quench your desires.

The approach to vertical calls to courage.

Let go, leave your fear behind.

Invite the call to grandeur,

Crossover...

Lift your feet and fly!

Compassion is Lighter

On your back, I learn how to fly.
It's easy, resting here in your beauty.

You carry sorrows from secrets unsaid,
a bending line between grief and joy.

Show me the sun, not the shadows
from the standard's doubt.

I know them too well.

Pausing at the peak of an arc,
I reflect no shadows,

no doubt.

This Changing Course

I feel you call and seven strides
turn to six. Majesty enters the arena,

a darkened line fades and turns to light.
In the distance a calling, a path that leads
our way to fate.

Hooves kiss the edge of the Liverpool where
clear water turns opaque. We pass

over sadness, that bears the weight of limitations.
Grand Prix rails seem level under our view as

we land inside a secret, where equine loving
takes form.

Seeds of Darkness

Blue ribbons soothe the soul,

but teach the mind nothing.

Your defeats are the wounds that serve you,

a course of rails are seeds of courage.

Falling rails turn the inside out,

showing you a hidden world.

Every shadow serves the sun,

not the other way around.

Look for shadows on the course of victory,

that darkness holds your light.

Everything Needs an Entry

The barn door opens,

and morning light comes in.

Two standards create a space,

a hole in the sky to enter.

Music isn't the rhythm of sounds,

it's the length of silence between the notes.

When we start to jump,

then our ladder arrives.

It's emptiness that clears the final rail,

not the wish for victory.

What Is

Grief comes, happiness happens.

That's just the way it is.

Rails fall, ribbons random.

Nothing you can do.

An honest horse, an honest woman.

Fate will find a way.

Calm and sunny, spooky horse.

That's just the way it is.

Never add to reality,

jump from the place where you know what is...

Is.

Send Me to the Bottom

Who turns tears to smiles?

When tears fall like rails, who moves the sun?

The only light not contained

under my saddle and in my soul.

There is rapture inside this arena,

a circling light inside fenced boundaries.

Who knows that fallen planks send me

to the bottom of the void to search for light?

Who knows the secret gifts of the universe?

Who frees my hope inside four faults?

The same circling light inside forgiveness.

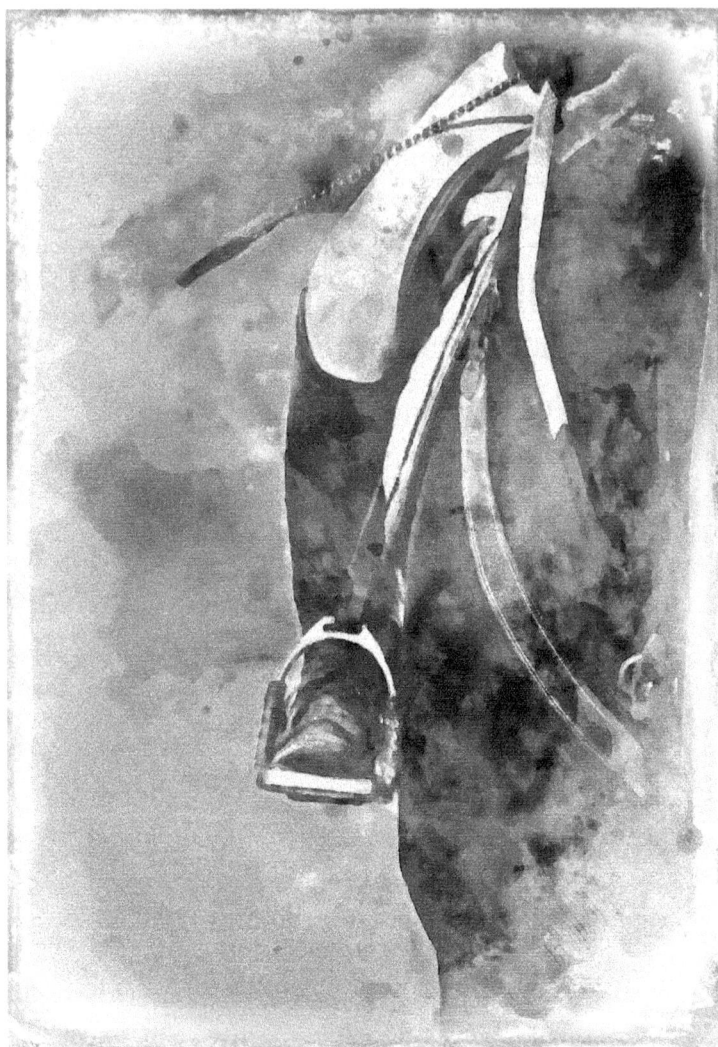

A Trainer's Wish

A horse jumping a meter fifty,
isn't looking for Grand Prix gold.

He's running just ahead of the rider's crop,
just in front of expectations.

A rider jumping over doubt,
isn't trying to win the event.

She is hoping for a safe return,
just behind her expectations.

There will always be another show,
questions and efforts made from fear.

Today you ride for love,
not the trainer's wish of expectations.

Bound Together

Stay with me friend,

what rises must fall.

Our friendship is bound

together by the depths of doubt.

When expectations fall, we break the

glass ceiling and rise above the last rail.

In our despair, the door opens

and hope comes flooding in.

Stay with me friend...

Here in this wakened moment.

Inside Doubt's Desire

You cannot break doubt's desire; it's the fear
that teaches you how to love. When you learn that,

you chase the fear that's chasing you. You
look to higher rails to face the face of fear.

Hesitation on the course of questions become
interpretation showing you the way. The whole
sky becomes the place you want to live.

Inside doubt's desire, inside equine love.

The Same Wind Blows

A tail looks beautiful in the wind,
the same wind blows a plank over
as hooves pass by.

A child loves the pony's courage,
it knows no limits of expectation.

A mind blows in the wind as
expectations fall short of its own limits.

Ride the expectations of a child over
the highest rails of fear to victory.

A Horse's Wish

Don't count on me.

Don't ride around the arena with

false notions of friendship.

Pay your own rent,

give what you can to the wind.

It's the only thing you have,

as it carries you over to victory.

When Separation Shatters

Stay with me. Never leave this circle of trust.

This is our life, this time between the efforts.

Never leave the arena to think of greener pastures;

that is only an illusion. Help me bow down,

just before a meter thirty.

Because I cannot go there alone.

This journey needs two, to break

the glass ceiling.

When separation shatters,

all the rest is love.

Judge the Jump

Inside of you is the queen's mare,

royal blood the color of gold.

Stop riding the peasant's nag,

sit in the presence of glory.

The pony's jump is a relative measure,

a child's victory, the smallest step.

You can win the Grand Prix,

but not reach Royalty.

Never judge the ride or rider,

judge the jump by the height of its majesty.

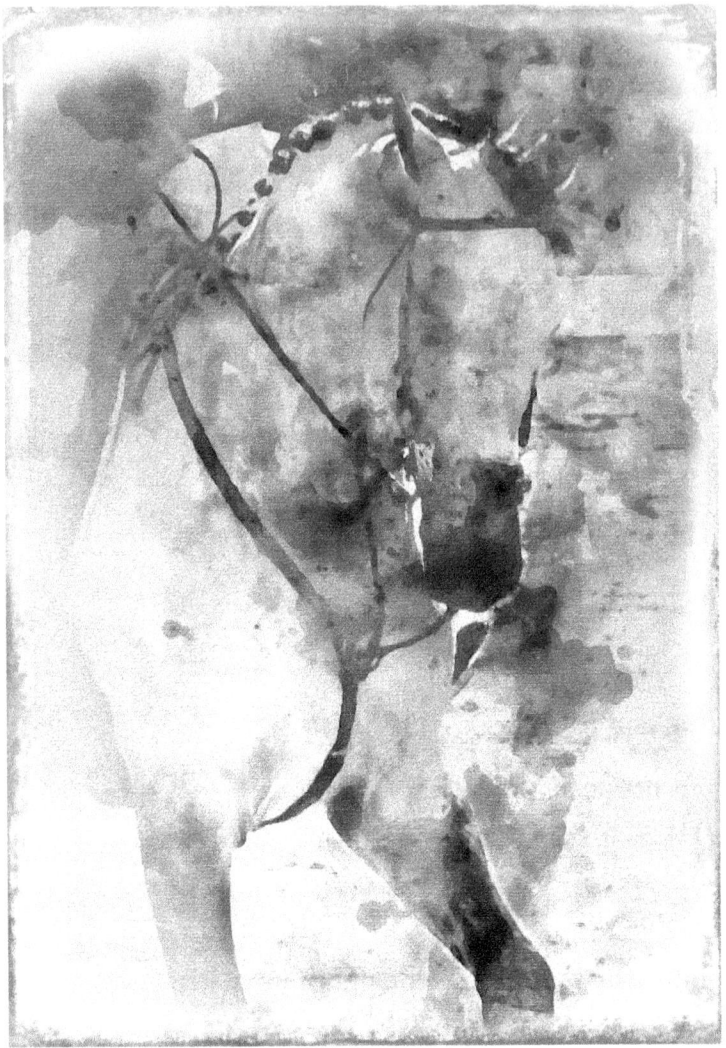

The Only Thank You That Hurts

We give thanks and keep this joy rolling. A pat on
the neck, a clenched fist high above the saddle.

The first jump a skinny vertical,
deep footing without any help.

The more we give thanks, the more rails
keep their place on the climb to gold.

Gratitude on short supply,
rails rain in stormy weather.

The second jump takes all my effort,
fast and flat is the wrong move here.

All I hear is the double buzzer-beep, beep.
The judge announces "Thank you rider."
As I leave the arena with the only thank you
that hurts.

Look Everywhere

Look at the essence of where the journey started,
every part, a part of the whole.

All things have a destination,
arriving from a source.

The answer serves the question,
not the other way around.

Every horse needs a rider,
the custom saddle is cut to fit.

Every course asks a question,
Can two hearts beat as one?

Without Thought

Today the footing is green, a garden
where human and horse meet.

When I sit in the saddle,
I feel courage coming in.

There is no hesitation, no distance
not found. I surrender to what is,
this equine soul in flight.

Without thinking, without ideas of
you and I. Without a vision of victory.

The only thing I hear is
the beating of an equine heart.

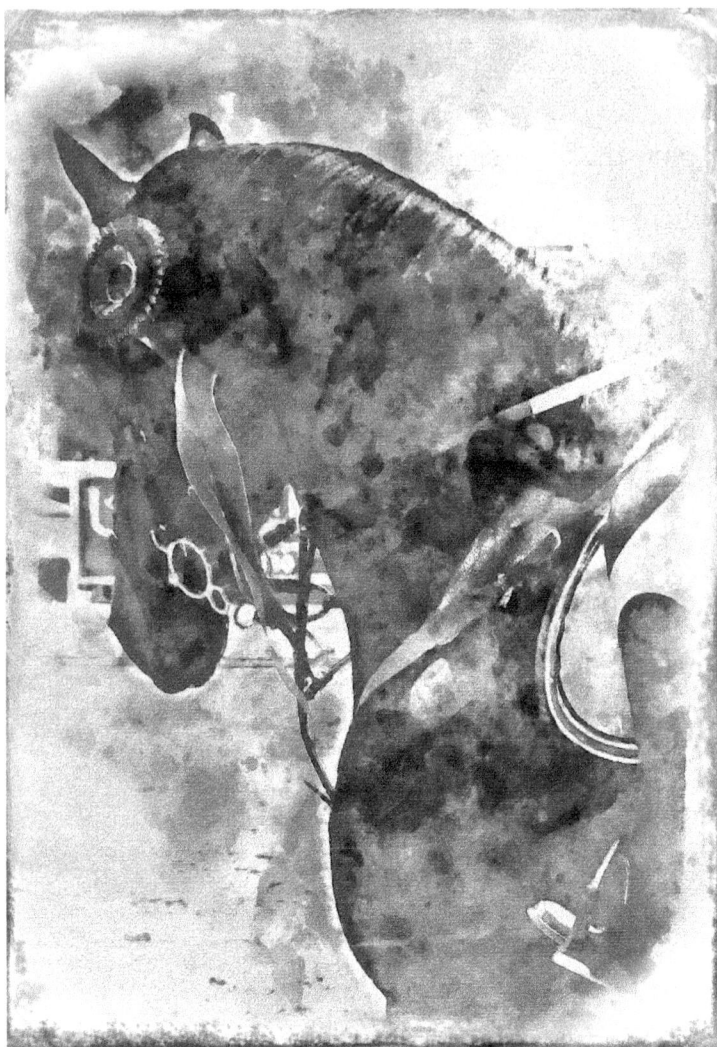

I Don't Want To Win

To be on top, well, that's O.K. sometimes.

But I would rather jump over first place,
landing in the middle where equine minds

lose all doubt somewhere between
too short and a little too long.

Another World

Who tells me to jump? Who sends the
message "NOW" is never too late?

I cannot tell you what the distance is,
yet I know the stride is four.

My horse clears a meter twenty,
but he has never thought of math.

Who broke this prison made of rails?
We punch a hole in the sky and find
another world.

Nothing up here but Silence,
the great shout of equine joy.

This Arena of Joy

When we enter the arena, there is
no room for fear.
This place is for union.

Let the sky and ground meet,
the horizon of victory. Let's jump
to the heights of love.

Leave our burdens behind, the sadness
that clings to life. When the sun shines
on darkness, all shadows flee.

We ride the lap of victory,
carried by equine joy.

Over These Rails

Over these rails, the view is different.

There is no worry up here on the back

of a trusted friend.

Over these rails, light dances to the tune of harmony.
Colors blend to form a rainbow.

Over these rails, falling is the order of the universe;
as hope descends beyond the shadow of doubt.

Over these rails, the sky holds a special

place where horse and human meet.

Over these rails.

The Soul's Enigma

This arena devours us with faults,
we saddle up to ride through the hesitation

and feed our souls. Who sent us here
to saddle up with hope and ride the

broken clay? Our souls answer the enigmas
of life by saying yes to each other. This invisible

game of despair works it's magic by leading us
to the hope of clean rounds. Where we die in the
light of emptiness.

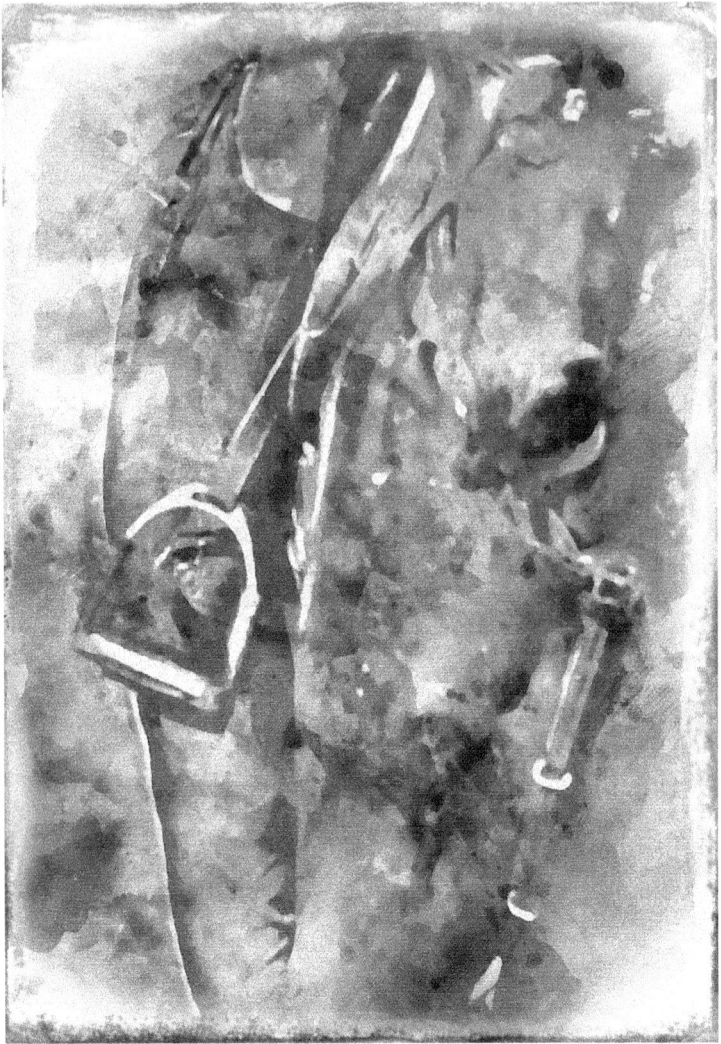

All I See

A lifted fist is the sign of victory,
a lifted tail, a sign of cramps.

A fallen comrade is the sign of battle,
a fallen rail, a sign of fear.

These things ebb and flow. Waves on a
beach kiss another storm goodbye.

Riding the storm; I sit in the saddle.
All I see is love... the sign of friendship
between horse and rider.

Between you and I.

An Equestrian Favor

As I enter the arena, this saddle carries a heavy load.

These shoes I have aren't made

to support this emotional weight.

There is no freedom when

my shoes are stuck in the ground.

When others watch us jump,

they wish they could ride with me.

They see the heights,

not the essence of the ride.

They should walk a mile in my shoes,

then they would understand.

A negative state pulls you to the earth.

Release me from this gravity prison,

    and together we can fly.

Facing Each Other

Sitting on this equine presence,
I feel the power of a trusted friend.

With no more questions, a course full
of friendship offers only answers.

Mind games turn inside out as
we climb this ladder of sky.

We cross over rails where no doubt can follow,
this place inside of hope.

Limitations kneel, as we turn to face
each other inside this upside-down sky.

Confusing Faith

Too much scope, and not enough faith.

The body can jump, but the spirit can soar.

The way to freedom is not a trainer's quip.

The height is cleared, but the heart left behind.

A cleared rail is a physical success,

the joy of youth, a passing moment.

A momentary success will give relief.

Only full commitment brings equine joy.

I See

On the front side of rails, all I see is doubt.

You see hope on the back side of flight.

With every stall door open,

you know the way home.

I need the right-hand red flag,

to see my way through.

You find answers without concern for thought,

I look at questions searching for a clue.

I see the depths of the Liverpool, as you walk

on water without a ripple.

I search for blame when doubt fills my mind,

you jump for joy all the way to victory!

Receiving Courage

You are hope at the end of a clean round,
music in the wind of a mane, clear sight

at the bottom of a pit. "How many strides to
the next effort?" is not a question for you. You

send echoes back to the heart's abyss, receiving
silence from the depths. Sitting in the saddle

my soul overlooks your poll. Receiving courage,
I search this puzzling course.

Jumping clear of all doubt.

Marc Ness was born in Billings, Montana, and received his education from Montana State University, where he earned a bachelor's degree of science in psychology. He has a personal interest in mysticism and poetry. He has an affinity for horses and enjoys the outdoors. He lives in Denver, Colorado.